Clifton King

writing poems in the sunlight

Royale Road Publishing, Carlsbad, California

writing poems in the sunlight

First Edition

Text Font: Times New Roman
Cover art: Claude Monet's *Impression Sunrise*

ISBN: 978-0-9786935-8-9

Library of Congress Control Number: 2021915558

Most of these poems were previously published in poetry books by this author: *Stolen Afternoons, Listen to the Tide, sand & water, Beach Bum, After a Summer Rain, Beachcombing.* A few of these poems first appeared in the *San Diego Poetry Annual* and *Summation,* and a few make their print debut here.

Printed in the United States of America

Royale Road Publishing, Carlsbad, California

for friends, family and you

Contents

Breathes there a bard who isn't moved
When he finds his verse is understood
And not entirely disapproved.
                              —Robert Frost

Monet's Garden

The garden is raucous with red and yellow.
Bees and butterflies are overwhelmed with choices.
I find a bench in the shade, try to imagine
Monet resting here all those years ago.
Today, gravel pathways crunch beneath a crush of tourists.
A muted mix of Italian, French, that proper King's English,
and the American version, fills fragrance laden air.

Nearby, a woman talks on her cell phone in French.
Her words, music I don't understand.
In the distance, school children play, raise a bouquet of laughter.
A girl, voice so soft I barely hear her request,
asks that I take her picture.

I intended to write a poem, share this garden with you, the reader.
Perhaps even mention Monet's house and beloved lily pond
just beyond those green garden gates.
But I see my lady coming down the path, sunlight in her hair.
She is the only poetry that interests me at the moment.
I will tell you about the garden later.

Love Poems

If my poems were strong enough,
each like the stones Jeffers gathered
alone the Carmel coast, I would build
a fortress where I could keep the world
at bay, away from our time together.
I could only hope the rain didn't find
those small crevices between my metaphors.
There would be an English garden out back.
I would paint the garden gate green,
if only for the alliteration.
And beyond the garden, the sea, all blustery
with whitecaps, dappled with the same blue
your eyes smile in the afternoon sun.
And from the forest of words that covers
those distant mountains I would harvest
love poems, lay them in the palm of your hand
                        —along with my heart.

Coming Home

I was born on a beach
just beyond the reach
of high tide. Yet,
I have not always been
a neighbor of the sea.
In those years that survived
my youth, mountains,
the color of freedom, bled rivers
into the valleys of my dreams.
And the same rain that fell
on ancient conifer forests
nourished the Oregon lifestyle.
But I was born on a beach
and have returned like
a spawning salmon
to end where I began.

A Woman's Eyes

Brown dominates worldwide, blue second.
My mother's eyes were blue; a blue
that could make a summer sky jealous.
I wonder my father's thoughts
when he first gazed into her eyes?

And there are large round brown eyes,
like those you find south of the border:
pleading eyes of hungry children, knowing
eyes of their mothers. And almond shaped eyes
like those of ancient Egyptian women who
accompanied the Pharaohs into the next world.

A woman's eyes are a mystery not easily solved.
And often, one glance is all it takes for a man
to make a complete fool of himself.

Poetry Book

It took years to compile these pages,
each word selected one at a time,
like Juan Valdez harvesting coffee beans.
It seems I did little else during those years.
Maybe that explains why my high school
sweetheart is now my ex-wife—maybe not.

Regardless of the cost, I have a book
of poetry. One might think fame and fortune
are in the near future. But, poets are a strange lot
unlike novelists and others who pen prose.
Poets must die, preferably by their own hand,
before fame finds them.

It took years to compile these pages. Yet who
will read them? Who buys poetry books?
In the bookstore customers will slide my book
from the shelf, browse its pages, then wedge me
back between all the other not-yet-dead poets.

It took years to compile these pages. If I had spent
that time on Wall Street learning the ins and outs
of hedge funds I could be driving a Rolls,
playing golf at the country club, living high
off other people's life savings.
But I chose the road less traveled.
Say......that's a good line.

Our Beach

A white belly of moon lingers
in the morning sky, the only
blemish on that pale blue abyss.
A sandpiper's scurry catches my eye,
that race to forage before the next
surge of sea. Above me gulls circle,
call the ocean by name. Sun warms
my shoulders, throws my shadow
down the beach. I hear your voice
in the song of waves, recall that day
you wrote my name in the sand.

Greenwich Village Wedding

There is no church,
no minster,
no gathering
of family and friends.

A tangled sheet
is her wedding gown,
that faux fireplace
their witness.

He whispers
I love you and *I do,*
in the same breath.

The red velvet wallpaper
proclaims,
You may kiss the bride.

Cowboy

The cowboy's gone you know. Oh, there's
still men raisin' cattle an' drivin' 'em to market.
But they're herdin' them steers with Jeeps,
an' ridin' fence in helicopters, then goin' home for supper.
An' they wear sunscreen an' Rayban sunglasses,
get Sundays off for church, an' a family Bar-B-Q.
They ain't cowboys. Not real cowboys.

An' there's city folk playin' at cowboyin'.
Anyone can do it, if 'n you got the money.
Jump a jet to Montana or Wyoming or Okalahoma,
slip into some tight britches an' a flannel shirt.
Don't forget the Stetson. Ride an' ol' swayback mare
behind a bunch a cows for an hour or so,
an' eat some bacon an' beans. Then schedule a massage
before the limo ride to the airport.
They surely ain't cowboys. Not real cowboys.

A cowboy sits a horse like he was born
in the saddle, leanin' into the Wyoming wind,
bandana high on his nose, hat pulled tight,
tipped into the dust churned by a thousand hooves.
His face, dark an' leathery from the Arizona sun,
eyes clear and truthful as winter air sweepin'
down through Colorado.

A cowboy walks like he's still in the saddle,
that silver jangle from his boots. He smells
of sweat an' wet horse flesh, an' chewin' tobacco.

A cowboy talks to his horse durin' the day,'
an' serenades the cattle at night, while sittin'
'round the campfire, boilin' coffee, an' watchin'
mesquite smoke mingle with the stars.

Yeah, the cowboy's gone—but his ghost rides
the Chisholm Trail, stirrin' up dust 'tween
Abilene an' Red River. An' he can be found
in most any cattle town from Cheyenne to
Wichita, Denver to Dodge.

So, if you're over that way, you may feel the ground
tremble, an' smell cattle an' horses an' men,
hear the squeak of leather on leather, saddles an' chaps,
an' rawhide ropes, an' the hollow beat of hooves.

An' if you wait 'till sundown, 'till the trail is black,
an' listen with a keen ear, you might hear the moans
of cattle an' the melody of cowboy ballads
in the lonesome prairie night—you might,
but you know—the cowboy's gone.

Proposition

Come with me to Paris,
where food is a religion,
love affairs short lived
as clean sheets in a bordello.
I'll buy you the Eiffel Tower
or maybe your own bridge
on the River Seine. We'll stroll
the boulevard, watch artists
struggle with color and light.

But here, in this California
beach town, all I can offer
are craggy coastal bluffs,
a stretch of sand stippled
with impressions of lovers
and the blood of a setting
sun spilled across the sea.
The only Parisian pleasure
I can promise is a French kiss.

Office

My office has a window that welcomes
the ocean breeze, and at night, when traffic
on 101 has died down, that song of waves
finding a cobbled shore waltzes in. I have
a swivel chair like a government official,
an in and out box filled with papers
that are neither coming nor going.
On my desk, a pair of carved horse head
book ends that were my mother's favorites.
But why does someone who is retired
have an office you might ask. Because,
every man needs a place to do business.
Mine is the business of poetry.
And let's not mistake *doing business*
with *making a living*. Poetry pays only
in the self-satisfaction of words on a page,
in that polite applause after reading
to a room of fellow poets who are only there
for the open mic. True, I don't really need
an office to write poetry. Yet, I need someplace
for that four-drawer file cabinet where I keep
all those poetry magazine rejection letters.

Response to William Carlos Williams

This Is Just To Say   by William Carlos Williams

I have eaten
the plums
that were in
the icebox

and which
you were probably
saving
for breakfast

Forgive me
they were delicious
so sweet
and so cold

I Must Say   by Clifton King

I am disturbed
by the thought
of eating plums
kept in an icebox

as the flesh
of fresh fruit
should
tease the tongue

like
that warm welcome
of a woman's
mouth

Dove Eggs

A mourning dove is nesting
in a hanging plant that sways
with each whisper of sea breeze.
A week ago, there were two eggs.
Then the crow that lives in a palm
down the street swooped in, wings
flared, menacing beak agape.
Mother dove flew off in fright.
I grabbed a broom as if I could
sweep away the danger. The crow
laughed as he carried off an egg.
I stood guard for hours, broom
at the ready. Finally, mother dove
returned, a surprised look on her
face when she saw only one egg.
I check on her daily, not that I can
prevent nature's course. I'm glad
humans don't prey on each other
like animals...........Oh, wait.

Sunday Ride

When you ride a motorcycle
it's not important the roads you travel
lead to where you are going.

The back road to Laguna Beach
snakes through Silverado Canyon
where clusters of small cabins
cling to hillsides, hidden
by a camouflage of trees and shadow.
You carve your way down the valley,
attack each turn, lean deep, defy gravity
and common sense. Your foot pegs
leave long scars in the pavement.
That staccato rasp of straight pipes
hangs in the air as you dash
through tunnels of shade,
flash across plateaus of sunlight.
Then, just as sudden as death itself,
clouds erase the sky and rain falls.
That double yellow becomes slick
as a used car salesman. Raindrops
sting like gravel tossed from heaven.
You creep into Laguna Beach,
find a Laundromat, strip down
to your boxers. There you stand,
a skinny, shivering, seventeen-year-old,
wondering what might happen
should someone come in to do laundry.

At Our Beach

I sit with sun on my face,
realize the glow I feel
comes from my thoughts of you.

I wonder how long
I've given the sun credit
for the warmth of our love?

A woman
who loves a woman
is forever young.
      —Anne Sexton

_____

Color

Blackbird fly, Blackbird fly
Into the light of the dark black night.
The Beatles

She was a girl I could have loved:
slender and dark, eyes the color
of a moonless night.

But it was 1962 and there were
some things society didn't want
a couple like us to do.

Father took me aside and said,
Son, life is like a painting. Select
colors for your canvas carefully.

I told him I wanted the world
to see her color, each brush stroke,
every swirl of the palette knife.

Still, in my heart I knew there were
some things society didn't want
a couple like us to do.

It was a November night when she
came to me, tearful and trembling,
to say she was going away.

She was a girl I could have loved.
But my blackbird took flight,
lost forever to that dark black night.

Beachcombing

An ebb tide leaves behind
those worthless passengers
of storm-tossed waves:
sinewy strands of seaweed,
shells and bits of driftwood.

I think of all I left behind.

I find a stone, smooth as a child's
face, flat as the earth before Aristotle.
I skip it across the shallows,
continue my search for something
I won't know until I see it.
That's the way of beachcombing
                       —and love.

Windbells and Children

Our windbell hangs from a porch beam, prompted
into song by ocean breezes, storm whipped winds
and on occasion it seems to sing out on its own.
It was an anniversary gift from our son's then girlfriend.
She is now, like yesterday's wind-bell song, in the wind.
This bronze bell is one-of-a-kind, born of fire, hammer
and anvil in Cosanti's* foundry. Each bell a descendent
of Paolo Soleri's vision. The bell's unique tone reminds
me of my children; lives gone different directions, forged
by the same hand and vision, sent out into the world
to find their place, sing their song.

*Cosanti, located in Paradise Valley, Arizona, is the headquarters,
 foundry, studio, and gallery for Paolo Soleri bronze & ceramic
 windbells & sculptures. Cosanti is a nonprofit educational
 organization dedicated to architectural research.

Ashes
— for Jeff

Tomorrow, when I see the new blue
of morning sky, feel sun on my face,
I will think of you old friend,
all those hours we spent watching
the horizon, waiting on that perfect
wave, holding on to life.
And then breakfast at The Deli:
coffee, bacon and eggs seasoned
with stories of long-ago travels;
afternoons in your living room,
dogs sprawled on the couch, and you
content in that canine clutter. But
your trips to the hospital scared the hell
out of me. How I admired your courage.
So tomorrow, when I see that new
morning sky, feel the sun's warmth,
I will think of those last minutes
I spent with you old friend
that day in La Jolla Cove when we
let you go, a swirl of ashes, a spirit
who couldn't wait to return to the sea.

Tulip Fields in Holland
from a poetry workshop

A Monet print hangs
on the far wall
of the reading room
in the public library.
Shards of sunlight slip
through the window.
A dance of shadows
from a eucalyptus
plays across the canvas.
The red and yellow
pigment tulips sway
in the changing light.
The windmill turns.
Water flows into the field.
Clouds drift through
a China blue sky.
We have ten minutes
to work on a poem.
I've forgotten the prompt,
wonder what to write about.

The Porch

I bought this house for the porch,
open to the west toward the Pacific.
Ocean breezes curl above the railing
and nudge our wind-bell into song.
This neighborhood is a bit older
than I'd like. (But then, so am I.)
Evenings I wrap myself in the quiet,
a security blanket worn thin by the years.
This old porch is more than concrete
and wood, brick and mortar.
This porch is a day at the beach,
a night in the desert, an afternoon
in a lover's bed. It's a trip down PCH
in that fast lane of my youth, the first
girl I kissed, that day I filed for divorce.
This porch is the morning my mother
died, our Paris apartment, that train
trip we didn't take to England.
It's the evening my daughter was born,
my first and last day of college,
all those skipped classes in between.
This old porch is our day in Central Park,
Strawberry Fields and Yoko's apartment.
It's Monet's lily pond, my bronzed
baby shoe perched on the bookcase,
our wedding day. This old porch
is that Harley I rode too fast, the first
time I held my granddaughter,
the last time I saw my father.
This old porch is you and me
together in that warm wind of life
flying our love like a kite.

Double Overhead

Waves are not measured in feet and inches,
they are measured in increments of fear.
                                Buzzy Trent

Somewhere, in a place as distant
as childhood, storms stir the sea.
Mountains of turquoise and cobalt
rise up like villains in a Grimm fairy tale.

On a morning so bright you forget
it is January, you paddle out
as you have a thousand times before.

Those first dark lines appear on the horizon:
furrows on the forehead of the world.

You race toward them, pray you find refuge
in deep water beyond towering crests,
that silent violence beneath their collapse.

Immortality rides the faces of these waves.
You believe in yourself, call it wisdom,
though from shore it looks like suicide.

You commit, let the sea swallow you
as you stretch a scar of your passage
across her swollen belly.

Life stampedes through your chest.
This is the way you want to die.

Down PCH on a '59 Triumph

My hobby, or what I do in my spare time,
is motorcycle.   James Dean

I'm seventeen years old.
The rasp of a British twin fills the air.
The highway is fog-bound, my tee-shirt
plastered to my chest, rivulets of moisture
crawl across the lenses of my sunglasses.
That youthful certainty of immortality
won't allow me to wear a helmet.
Wind ties my long, sun-bleached hair
into knots as the mechanical beast
beneath me eats asphalt at an alarming rate.
The cacophony of howling tires,
valve clatter, slap of primary chain
and of course, that desperate scream
of an engine with straight pipes
takes me to a high second only
to the raw, fear awakening acceleration.
And that girl on the back, arms wrapped
tightly around me, shouts, *I love you.*
But I know it's the adrenaline of speed,
that unspoken presence of danger talking.
I know it's the motorcycle.
And that's okay with me.

Your Name

I spend the morning
at our beach
where the sky
is a collage
of confused clouds,
the ocean dappled
with only a thought
of whitecaps,
and a breeze
that whispers
your name.

Greener Days

A lone tree stands
on a bluff above the Pacific.
Bent from the constant caress
of an ocean breeze,
branches bare, stark
against an ever-changing coastal sky,
not a single leaf or bud
with the promise of new life.
When I was a younger man
it was green with creation
and threw shade across
purple blossoms that crowded
the ground around it.
I would unfold my beach chair,
sit in its shadow, write poetry,
never a thought of that tree
becoming nothing more
than deadwood, or of me
growing into an old man
remembering greener days.

Tuesday Walk

A sunhat shaded your face.
Yet, your eyes beamed like sunlight.
Flowers in your garden
seemed to sing with your every touch.
The sky was uncluttered, just blue,
like the first day of Creation.
It was a Tuesday, not unlike
any other day of the week—until you.

Indian Beach

A slice of wild Oregon coast,
wide, windswept,
dotted with tide pools.
Sea stacks
rise from the ocean.
We travel the road in,
long and winding,
meandering
beneath a canopy
of coast range forest
thick with evergreens,
carpeted in ferns.
Offshore,
Tillamook Rock Lighthouse
still stands guard
in an oft angry sea.
And in a light summer rain
I kiss her the first time.

Half Mast

Old Glory flies at half mast.
Not a whisper of wind.
Like a head hung low
in heartbreaking sorrow,
stars and stripes drape lifeless
against the flagpole.
This display of grief and respect
is for a former President.
Yet, it's become too common
a sight: flags flying at half mast
for students massacred
in their classrooms,
for innocent people
slaughtered in God's house,
for celebrators murdered
in theaters and nightclubs.
Flags, soaked in tears,
fly at half mast. Yet,
our outrage is ignored,
hollow condolences
handed out like campaign promises.

Buffalo

I am Buffalo.
In the days after the first moon
I was thunder across the prairies,
a pageant of dust that settled on the sun.
I was as many as the blades of grass,
the earth trembled beneath my hooves.
Long before this land had a name
the Indian came and we were brothers.
He took what he needed, nothing more.

I am Buffalo.
My brother danced and sang my name
in his lodge, painted his face for the hunt.
I gave myself, my flesh for food, my hide
for warmth, my bones for tools.
Glorious death, then I lived forever in legend.
Buffalo. I was revered

—until the Anglo.
You came with horses and guns,
your ignorance and greed.
I ran from your bullets but you killed me
again and again,
ripped the hide from my carcass,
left my flesh to rot in the sun;
prairie red with blood,
the stench of slaughter.

You killed me to starve the Indian.
You killed me for sport
from your iron horse.
You killed me and laughed,
to impress a woman,
to win a bet, to pass the time.
You murdered me,
and never gave it a thought.

I am Buffalo.
Never again will the thunder be heard,
the earth tremble, the sun fade
in the sod churned by multitudes.
Now you struggle to rescue me
from your own hand.

I am Buffalo.
Back from the grave,
from the mountains of bleached bones,
back from the slaughter.

     Not because I am revered.
     Not because we are brothers.
     But because, you are ashamed.

Endow the living with the tears
You squander on the dead…
—Emily Dickinson

Hume Lake, 1963

We take Forest Service road 30.
Miles of dusty gravel ruts lead us
to Hume Lake nestled within
the Sierra Nevada. A green blanket
of pine trees covers the hillsides,
creeps down to water's edge.
Ducks glide along the placid surface.
An eagle's cry echoes down
a shallow canyon that cradles
Tenmile Creek, holds it captive
behind an old concrete dam.
We find a secluded inlet. Clothes
fall to the ground like oak leaves
in autumn. Our hearts race with
the embrace of mountain cold water,
then again when we make love,
afternoon sun warm on our bodies.

A Morning at Ponto Beach

Pelicans sprawl across a blue collage
of sky: a lazy line unlike those sharp
vees of migrating ducks and geese.

They dip low over the sea, mirrored
in her glassy surface, wing in unison,
then glide—wing, glide—wing, glide.

I wonder if the last in line
calls out the rhythm, the pace,
like a coxswain in a racing shell.

I listen, hear only silence,
that occasional surrender of waves.

Now, the pelicans are gone,
disappeared from sight in the time
it took me to write these few lines,

much the way life slips away
while we are busy with something else.

Needs

I cannot exist on words alone.
I need a bright morning
with a sliver of late moon,
sun rising yellow, setting orange;
butterfly wings, hummingbird beaks;
daffodils, dusty miller blossoms.

I need a sky clear blue, cloudy gray,
mid-day blaze of white, shadows
under foot; palm fronds
for an island hut roof; an old
pair of shoes; a new dog.

I need the sea, calm and glassy,
windswept and rough; nights
bedazzled with neon and starlight.

I need the touch of a woman,
the love of a woman.

I need you.

Addiction

That weekend chaos on Pacific Coast Highway rumbles
passed as I stand at the edge of a bluff above the Pacific.
Below, a thread of beach stretches along the California coast.
It is overrun by the multitudes escaping inland heat.
The vivid reds, blues and greens of beach umbrellas
and sunshades smear the sand with a collage of color
like an impressionist painting. This façade disappears
into that distant haze regurgitated from the LA basin.
The ocean today is lake-like, calm, well mannered,
nearly silent where sea meets sand. The pungent
aroma of rotting, fly infested, seaweed mingles
with the sweet scent of sunscreen and hibachi smoke.
Small children at water's edge scream and laugh
with the pure joy of cold ocean water swirling
around their ankles. Most men and women on the beach
are attired in swimwear they really should reconsider.
But, I'm not here to judge. I'm here for my ocean fix.
I take a hit of sea breeze, drop a little summer sky,
mainline this late June sun and that lazy line of pelicans.

Cruisin' the '55

I invite her into my fictitious '55 Chevy
for a cruise around the living room,
no plans to go any farther. Yet,

there is something in her laugh,
the way she touches my hand
and that look in her eyes

when she realizes I want her.
So, we drive down a different road,
travel back to those yester-years

of drive-in movies, the riddle
of how to finesse that first kiss
and that lurid call of the back seat.

Ponto Beach on a Big Day
knowing your limits

I walk across a Monday morning beach
stippled with weekend footprints.
A bitter breeze blusters out of the north,
siphons off an early sun's warmth.
I stumble across a railroad tie half buried
in the sand, splintered, nearly unrecognizable.
The sea is not kind to accidental travelers.
Fifty feet from water's edge lies a long scar
of cobbles, some the size of a three-month-old
bar of hand soap, others the size of your fist,
all smooth, rounded from eons of tumbling
in the surf before being stranded.

I fix my gaze on the sea, toward the horizon
where the ocean rises up, where surf is born.
Today, storm tossed, eight feet at least.
I watch incoming swells, imagine how
I might position myself to catch a ride.
There, just left of that peak. Paddle hard.
The tail of my board lifts slightly. I drop in.
A sweeping bottom turn and I find the sweet spot.
I take a few steps toward the nose. More speed.
Mother Nature carries me in silent liquid flight.
The wave towers just above my head.
I catch a rail and the ocean devours me.
The sea is beautiful, but unforgiving and violent.
I will paddle out tomorrow. Today I just watch.
It's taken me nearly 80 years to learn my limits.

The Nature of Love

I recall those hours
we first roamed free
in the valleys,
across the plateaus
of our bodies;
how we pushed
against each other
like continental plates
that birth earthquakes
and tsunamis.

I can still hear
those small sounds
that flew
from your mouth
like hummingbirds
and hovered
in candlelit bedroom air,
spirits of our love affair.

Last Will & Testament

To my children:

I will leave nothing
I will take it all with me
I will take man's inhumanity to man
I will take terrorism, war, and those who wage it
I will take greed, stupidity, insensitivity
I will take politicians, liars, cheats
I will take hunger, poverty, illiteracy   .
I will take murder, rape, incest
I will take tyranny, bigotry, cruelty
I will take cancer, AIDS, every affliction known
I will take what was left to me—with me

Limits

Our limits are often set by others:
our speed rolling down PCH,
the number of checks you can write
without a service charge, the amount
of data available on your phone plan.
Some limits we place on ourselves when
common sense overrides testosterone:
admit when the surf is too gnarly,
a white shark sighting too recent.
So, we stay in our favorite beach chair,
listen to the constant music
of the Pacific Ocean, question why
seagulls gather on the sand,
always face into the wind
like a flock of weathervanes.

Long Beach State, 1961

Sue is a surfer from Ventura.
She has straw colored hair, a smile
that raises my blood pressure. Her
eyes, the color of that seldom seen
green flash, dance when she speaks.
Flawless skin glows a deep tan,
like coffee with too much cream.
A slight smear of pink lipstick
adorns her mouth. We meet most
mornings in the college parking lot;
our token effort at attending classes.
More days than not, we choose now
over the future. My old Chevy
spews blue smoke as we head
for Seal Beach, five miles down PCH.
The campus, perched on a green hillside
with its web of walkways, its halls
of learning, fades in the rear-view mirror,
along with our collegiate careers.

Insurmountable

I have been to the mountain,
to her meadows that lie quietly
in the foothills, walked through
valleys of wildflowers, listened
to that soft song of the lark.
I have been to the mountain,
struggled up slopes of shale,
fought for footing in rubble
as ancient as time itself, only
to dream of early meadow days.
I have been to the mountain,
confronted treacherous granite
cliffs where the eagle's call
was the only voice to be heard.
I have been to the mountain
but could not reach the summit
no matter which words I spoke,
no matter what concessions I made,
no matter how many times I prayed.
I have been to the mountain
but she would not embrace me.
So, I have returned to the sea.

Questions

I wonder about the seagulls.
How do they know when
a minus tide will expose
mussels that cling
to these jetty boulders?
Do they read the same
tide charts I do?
And when did they learn
to open those shells
held together as tightly
as a child's hands in prayer?

Finding an *I Love You*

I toss an *I love you* into the sea,
hope it returns on the changing tide.
The sun slips silently below the horizon
to become someone else's sunrise.
Our sky darkens to the purple of night.
Stars fall on the ocean. Their fire floats
next to a pale sliver of new moon,
neither as bright as your eyes. I find
yesterday's *I love you* washed ashore,
tangled in the tail of a shooting star.
Unable to separate them I bring both
home, a gift to go with all those others:
the unbroken shells, rocks that shimmer
when wet but become pallid as they dry,
pieces of driftwood, chunks of fallen trees,
bits of bamboo and every *I love you*
I ever offered up in your name.

Saturday Auction

My ol' truck just couldn't make it
from town to the ranch,
so I pulled in at Charlie's Auction Yard
to let 'er cool down, like I did most every
Saturday afternoon. I cussed an' kicked
the running board, then wandered out back
where they keep the livestock.

First time I saw her, I knew she was something special.
She wasn't the prettiest, that ol' buckskin Mare,
standing alone in the auctioneer's pit.
Just a wore-out ol' saddle bronc.

I could see right off, she'd been rode hard over the years,
them scars, up an' down her neck and shoulders,
from cowboy spurs, jabbin' an' slicin' for decades,
eight seconds at a time.

And that look in her eyes, like she don't trust no one.
But she held her head high, kinda proud like,
and the way she moved, muscled an' smooth,
I was pretty cert'n she was more than
just some ol' rodeo horse, that couldn't
make the next call to the chute.

They called her number, but she balked
when the cowboy tried to lead her in,
pullin' hard again' the reins and rearin' her head,
like she knew this was the end of the line.

The auctioneer began his song, the numbers
weren't big, and there weren't many takers.
Just a fat man that runs a rodeo south of the border.
And the guy from the slaughterhouse,
smokin' a big cigar, makin' his bid without even lookin'.
Just eight hundred pounds of dog food to him.

The auctioneer sang out,
I got one-seventy-five, do I hear one-eighty?
The only sound —
that ol' Mare pawin' at the concrete floor.
Goin' once!
Goin' twice!

Then I heard the bid, *Three hundred dollars!*
I turned to see who the fool was, and realized
it was me.
I didn't have but two hundred on me,
but they took my word and a handshake for the rest.

She ain't had a buckin' strap or a cowboy on her back since.
I never did give her a name, just call her Ol' Gal,
figure she don't mind.
To this day, I don' know why I bought that ol' saddle bronc.
Some things you do—just 'cause it feels right.

Royale Road Publishing, Carlsbad, California